Life's Wisdom

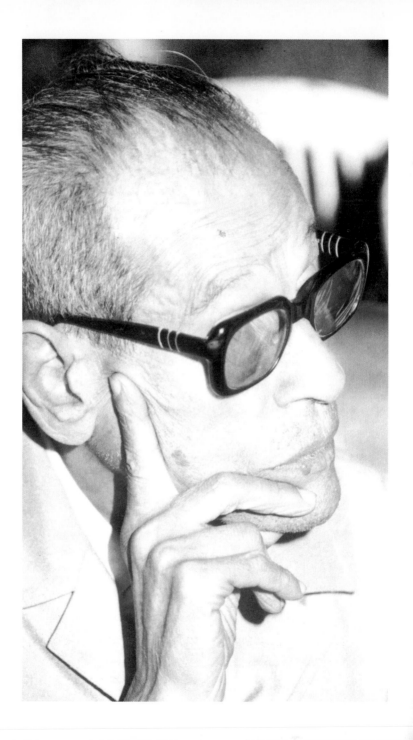

Life's Wisdom

from the Works of the Nobel Laureate

Naguib Mahfouz

Edited by Aleya Serour

The American University in Cairo Press
Cairo ❧ New York

Dar el Kutub No. 2256/06
ISBN 977 416 020 7

Designed by Andrea El-Akshar
Printed in Egypt

Contents

Foreword

by Naguib Mahfouz

I am very grateful to al-Sitt Aleya—Aleya Serour—whom I have had the pleasure of knowing and working with for some quarter of a century, for her excellent idea of pulling out the cream of my thoughts from my collected works and for her hard work in reviewing and re-reading all my books and bringing together the material collected here in this volume. This is the first time anyone has undertaken such a compilation from my writings, and I feel sure that her gleanings, based on her own point of view, will form an intriguing summarization of my thoughts and world-view over sixty years of writing. I hope that when all my friends around the world read these selections they will appreciate the great work that al-Sitt Aleya has done, and I wish her and the American University in Cairo Press, and this book, continued success.

نجيب محفوظ

Editor's Introduction

"When I chose writing as my career, the decision was irrevocable. There was no question of simply trying one thing instead of something else, with a view of giving it up if something more appealing came along. It was a choice for life." These are the words of Naguib Mahfouz, Egypt's Nobel laureate for literature in 1988, who has written over thirty-five novels and more than fifteen collections of short stories, as well as numerous screenplays for films (though none of those were for the many films made of his own works). It is from the English translations of his works that have been published by the American University in Cairo Press during his long writing career that the quotations in this little book—*Life's Wisdom*—have been drawn.

Naguib Mahfouz was born on 11 December 1911, in Gamaliya, an old quarter of Cairo on which he has drawn heavily for the setting of many of his novels. In an interview with the Associated Press in 1994, commenting on his novel *Midaq Alley,* which is set in that area, he said the alley "may be small, but it is large in my heart." The alley has played an important part in most of Mahfouz's works, although his first published novel, *Khufu's Wisdom* (1939), was set in pharaonic Egypt, as were his following two novels, *Rhadopis of Nubia,* and *Thebes at War.* His most popular work is *The Cairo Trilogy,* which consists of *Palace Walk* (for which he received the State Prize for Literature in 1957), *Palace of Desire,* and *Sugar Street.* Mahfouz then turned to the realistic novels of the sixties, *The Thief and the Dogs, Autumn Quail, The Search, The Beggar, Adrift on the Nile,* and *Miramar.* He then wrote the episodic novels *Mirrors, The Harafish, Arabian Nights and Days,* and *The Journey of Ibn Fattouma.* These are only a selection of the titles published in English translation by the AUC Press. His latest work, *Ahlam fatrat al-naqaha,* which first appeared in 2003, was published in English in 2004 under the title *The Dreams.*

Mahfouz started writing early, while still in primary school. In high school and during his university years he published a number of articles in newspapers and magazines. He studied philosophy at what is now Cairo

University, graduating in 1934. He worked as a civil servant in several government organizations, including Cairo University, the Ministry of Endowments, and the Ghuri library near Gamaliya, and later as director of the Foundation for the Support of Cinema. Before his retirement in 1971 he worked as consultant on cultural affairs to the Ministry of Culture. During this period he also found ample time to read and write.

In the book *Naguib Mahfouz at Sidi Gaber*, he offers these views about writing: "The writer must learn from his predecessors' experience. If he does not, he will remain a prisoner of the confines of his own imagination. . . . General knowledge is the raw material from which they will draw their inspiration, the petri dish in which their creativity can coalesce and bring forth a crystallized element of truth and beauty." Again he says: "Literary writing is an art that focuses on the aesthetic above all else. Regardless of the social, political, or other subjects with which it deals, the content is always submerged within the formal qualities of the work. . . . A literary writer makes every effort to embellish and improve the word since such embellishment is part and parcel of the aesthetic of his working procedure." Literary writing with Mahfouz is not only "an art that focuses on the aesthetic," but it abounds in his philosophy and experience of life.

As indicated by the variety of his works, Naguib Mahfouz has probably made use of all the forms of the novel used by his predecessors, and I would go as far as to say that he has even invented new ones. His character portrayal is exceptional: famous characters such as al-Sayyid Ahmad Abd al-Jawad in *The Cairo Trilogy* are quoted to this very day. Mahfouz's style is just as varied as his form, and some of his passages verge on poetry.

My own acquaintance with Naguib Mahfouz began in the 1970s, when I started work at the AUC Press and the first contract, for the translation of two of his novels, was signed. This was followed the next year by another contract, for the translation of four of his works. Later, other contracts were signed and the AUC Press began publishing more and more of his works, the latest being this present volume. During all these years I have known Naguib Mahfouz and worked with him as his so-called 'literary agent,' a term then unknown to the Egyptian publishing scene. I was known to Mahfouz as 'al-Sitt Aleya' ('lady,' not in its grandiose sense, but equivalent to 'Ms.'), and he still calls me that. He would come every year to the AUC Press to ask "Where is al-Sitt Aleya?" and inquire about his royalties. This was my relationship with Mahfouz at that time.

It was in 1985 that the real breakthrough for the Press came when Mark Linz, the director, signed a foreign rights agreement with Mahfouz, whereby the AUC Press became the author's sole agent for all foreign-language rights. Three years later Mahfouz was awarded the Nobel prize for literature. At that time the Press had one agent in Switzerland for German rights, but with the overwhelming demand for translations, the Press immediately sold English-language rights to fifteen of his works (later to become twenty) in the United States and Britain to Doubleday, now a division of Random House. The Press then contacted agents for Scandinavian, Spanish, Italian, and French rights, while all other rights were handled directly by the AUC Press. Demand was so great that the director, his secretary, and I had to work weekends for a whole year to try to keep pace with the work, and all the English translations of Mahfouz had to be reprinted over and over again.

It was after he received the Nobel prize that I began to visit him regularly downtown at the Ali Baba Café, near the American University in Cairo, where he used to go every day for his morning coffee. He would walk from his apartment in Agouza (where he lives with his wife and two daughters), cross the Nile by the Qasr al-Nil bridge, and reach his favorite coffee shop, where he would always be at the same window seat overlooking al-Tahrir Square.

From 1988 onward Mahfouz was besieged, as was the AUC Press, with requests from foreign publishers for translations of his works. We would meet every day to discuss contracts, publishers' requests, letters, and fan mail, receive his replies to all these issues, and convey them on his behalf to the parties concerned. Besides, he was overwhelmed by reporters, both local and from abroad, eager to interview him. All this took up much of his time, but he felt it his duty, after receiving the Nobel prize, to meet and talk with all these people. This continued, though in a lesser degree, as the years passed by, and it was not until 1994, after being attacked and stabbed in the neck by a religious fanatic, that he was prevented from walking by himself to the Ali Baba Café. Fortunately Mahfouz survived, but the injury severely impaired the use of his right hand.

He continues to write to this day, although after the attack on his life, and with the onset of old age, he is too weak to write more than what he calls his "Dreams"—no more than a page each—which range from the short, short story to the reverie.

Life has changed for the famous writer, but he remains the same modest person, with his great sense of humor and unfaltering wit. By now, most of his works have been translated. Over four hundred different editions of his

works exist, translated into thirty-three languages that include English, Spanish, Dutch, Italian, Greek, Portuguese, Danish, Norwegian, Swedish, Finnish, and French, as well as Icelandic, Faroese, and Kazakh. The Swedish Academy of Letters said in its Nobel citation that Mahfouz "through works rich in nuance—now clear-sightedly realistic, now evocatively ambiguous—has formed an Arabic narrative art that applies to all mankind." And it is this universal appeal that has attracted such worldwide demand.

I may have known Naguib Mahfouz as a person—modest, quick-witted, humorous, gentle, kind—traits that all the people around him have come to know. But during the thirty or more years I have known him, I had little time to read more than four or five of his novels, and perhaps some of his short stories. It was not until I started working on this little, big book (big in the wisdom it contains), that I was astounded and fascinated by what I read. Not only by the different forms and styles, not only by his brilliant descriptions of places, and his extraordinary portrayal of characters, but by the philosophical content of his writings. They really were full of wisdom, and my admiration and appreciation of the writer has grown tenfold.

In his novel *Mirrors*, there is a description of the character Reda Hamada that reiterates what I find in

Mahfouz: "… a man of pure intentions, gentleness, sincere, faithful to principles—freedom, democracy, culture, a religious creed purged of fanaticism and superstition."

The present book is a distilled collection of quotations from this great author's works that clearly reflect his deep insights, philosophy, and views on themes such as youth, love, marriage, death, freedom, faith, and the soul: all the subjects that take us through life's journey.

Nadine Gordimer says in her introduction to Mahfouz's *Echoes of an Autobiography*: "The essence of a writer's being is in the work, not the personality, though the world values things otherwise, and would rather see what the writer looks like on television than read where he or she really is to be found: in the writings." This collection of quotations from his writings has been carefully selected to show "the essence of the writer's being."

To quote once more from Nadine Gordimer's introduction to *Echoes of an Autobiography*: "Whatever your personal hermeneutics, it is impossible to read this work without gaining, with immense pleasure and in all gratitude, illumination through a quality that has come to be regarded as a quaint anachronism in modern existence, where information is believed to have taken its place. I pronounce with hesitation: wisdom. Mahfouz has it."

Editor's Acknowledgments

I am extremely grateful to Mark Linz, Director of the American University in Cairo Press, for giving me the opportunity to compile this book; to Neil Hewison for his editorial comments; to Ibrahim Makami, for inspiring me to undertake the work; and to Noha Hefny for her support. Above all, my debt is to Naguib Mahfouz himself. It is his work, in all its variety, and in the inexhaustible richness of its philosophy, that forms the bedrock of this book.

Life's Journey

Time, sadly, moves always onward—never turning back!
And as it moves it delivers the destiny decreed for each
person, executing its will—whose alteration and
exchange are the sole comic diversion easing the bore-
dom of eternity. From it comes all that time decays, and
all that is renewed; all that revels in youth, and all that
moans with age unto its final demise.

Khufu's Wisdom

A child . . . leaves the stability of the womb for the chaos
of the world.

Palace Walk

School is . . . the factory that makes useful men out of boys.
The Time and the Place

When a child who has not started school yet hears a school bell ring, he smiles, but once he is a pupil it sounds like a warning of the many hardships ahead.
Palace Walk

When we were playful children, who would have ever dreamt that such would be our fate?
The Beginning and the End

Don't let the infant within you forget what strenuous chores your mother endures for the sake of your fun. She bears you in her womb for nine months, then she holds you close . . . feeding you with her milk. Do not annoy her, for the Lord hears her complaints, and answers her pleas.
Khufu's Wisdom

Youth, leisure, and worldly goods oft prove a man's undoing.
Miramar

Some people can live in this world, festering as it is with its bitter troubles, without either home, money, or friends, and know neither worry, grief, nor need.

Midaq Alley

How many a man has set out to climb a mountain and found himself descending into a deep chasm!

Thebes at War

Girls today no longer have the ability to get along with people. . . . Where are the ladies of yesteryear?

Palace Walk

Man is the product of the experiences through which he passes, though the impact of these experiences takes some time to surface.

Naguib Mahfouz at Sidi Gaber

Man's civilization is not determined by what he owns, but by the pulse of his thoughts and heart.

Mirrors

Never get too close to a man who hates himself.

Miramar

It is when a man is tested that he's honored or despised.

Palace Walk

Day after day, my faith confirms that man's purity is as much from outside as it is from inside, and that we must provide light and clean air if we want beautiful flowers.

Mirrors

A person in trouble who lacks an adequate line of defense will resort to humor in order to allow himself to escape in happy clamor rather than let himself be subjected to scorn and condescending laughter.

Palace Walk

Nations will be overthrown and eras will pass away. Yet the fates will always produce a woman going about her business and a man seriously pursuing her.

Sugar Street

You can rebuild a ruined house, but not a human being.
The Harafish

The young seek adventure, the old long for security.
Miramar

Nothing destroys a man like his own self. . . . And no one can save him like his own self.
Arabian Nights and Days

Only time can prove the true merits of men.
Akhenaten, Dweller in Truth

If men gave way to sorrow, they would collapse from the weight of their burdens.
Palace of Desire

Men only gain distinction by challenging difficulties.
The Harafish

Everything now has its value except human beings.
Mirrors

Men go, but their good deeds remain forever.
Respected Sir

There are men who say nothing but work silently.
Palace of Desire

A good man is a fortune in himself.
Miramar

Man shoulders the burden of humanity as a whole, or
else he is nothing.

The Beggar

Only men can ruin women, and not every man is capable
of being a guardian for them.

Palace Walk

Sometimes marriage comes without anyone referring to it, like death.

Adrift on the Nile

❧

Where does the good seed grow except in the good soil?
Khufu's Wisdom

❧

Why have people kept on getting married, then, since the beginning of creation?

Because warning and caution are futile for marriage as for death.

Palace Walk

❧

Marriage is the ultimate surrender in life's losing battle.
Sugar Street

❧

The virtue of marriage is that it takes care of one's lust and so purifies the body.

Khufu's Wisdom

Marriage is just a big deception. After a few months as tasty as olive oil, your bride turns into a dose of castor oil.

Palace Walk

There is nothing more miserable than having a son who's a disappointment.

Palace of Desire

A son's rebellion means endless sorrow.

The Seventh Heaven

It's only married men who complain about marriage.

Midaq Alley

If it weren't for children, no one would ever tolerate married life.

Sugar Street

⋇

A sincere husband is as faithful to his wife when he's away from her as when he's with her.

Palace Walk

⋇

Falseness in life is the secret that makes man's inner self a rare truth; it hides from him although it's obvious to all.

Mirrors

⋇

If we could judge people's hearts by comparison with a mother's, all others would seem to be stones.

Palace of Desire

⋇

Women's lack of ideology or philosophy proves that ideology and philosophy hinder real, vital activity. A woman is only concerned with creation and all things connected, she is a beautiful creator, and creation is the center of her life. All other activities are of man's making and are necessary for domination, not creation!

Mirrors

Women's liberation movements are essential components of any renaissance in a people's history. A society cannot renew itself unless this is accompanied by a movement to liberate women.

Naguib Mahfouz at Sidi Gaber

Woman is life, and in her presence Truth is crowned by Death itself with all Death's solemnity.

Respected Sir

Just as one can find a deviant housewife, there's an honorable working woman.

Mirrors

The desperate attempts of a drowning woman to rescue herself are as futile as a poor man's dream of happiness.

The Beginning and the End

The love of a woman is like political theater: there is no doubt about the loftiness of its goal, but you wonder about the integrity of it.

Adrift on the Nile

※

Women's liberation is not limited to equal rights and duties: it also implies their full participation in the political and economic as well as social and cultural spheres.

Naguib Mahfouz at Sidi Gaber

※

Woman . . . possessed an instinct which guided her in the knowledge of her most intimate affairs without recourse to the intellect; and if humanity as a whole had this sort of instinctive access to the unknown, it would not have remained unknown.

Respected Sir

※

Nothing can replace the tender love of parents.

The Journey of Ibn Fattouma

※

One really needs a mother and the special quality of the love only she can give. . . . I can't imagine what it must be like to grow up without that kind of tenderness—one must feel an aching void all one's life. . . . No one can really take a mother's place.

Naguib Mahfouz at Sidi Gaber

The world is a woman's goal and idol—in another sense, it's the goal of creation.

Mirrors

A woman without children is like wine without the power to intoxicate, like a rose without scent, or like worship without strong faith behind it.

Khufu's Wisdom

Men follow beautiful women wherever they are. This is a basic principal of life.

Midaq Alley

Exchanging love in an atmosphere of healthy frankness is better than suppression and traveling from the arms of one prostitute to another.

Mirrors

Woe to the person who suffers from old age and feeble-ness. These two weaklings shake the strongest giants!

Khufu's Wisdom

The lucky ones are those who never grow old.

The Harafish

One can never wipe out the past; it goes on with the future.

The Beginning and the End

A man's nature softens as the years advance.

Khufu's Wisdom

What good is remorse after eighty?

Miramar

The Passing Game

❧

When I went to Alexandria by train, I would always get off at Mahattat Masr, the last station on the line. So when I passed Sidi Gaber station I could afford the comfort of knowing that I wasn't getting off quite yet. But I also knew that I was edging closer and closer to Mahattat Masr, that it wouldn't be long before I had to pack my luggage and get ready to exit the train.

Naguib Mahfouz at Sidi Gaber

❧

This is life. Painful though it is, the members of every family are eventually bound to part happily from one another, for each has his or her own role to perform in life.

The Beginning and the End

Some of the lies of life spurt forth in truth.
Echoes of an Autobiography

Why isn't life made up of perpetual days of courtship?
The Time and the Place

A life is not judged by its length.
Palace of Desire

Nothing lasts forever, neither sorrow nor joy. We have to go on living. When hard luck leads us down a closed path, we have to look for another.
Miramar

With every mounting crisis comes relief.
The Day the Leader Was Killed

Why do we not record the sweet avowals . . . so that they may be of benefit to us in the hour of dryness?
The Time and the Place

How can we turn life into a perpetual state of intoxication without resort to alcohol? We won't find the answer through debate, productivity, fighting, or exertion. All those are means to an end, not an end in themselves. Happiness will never be realized until we free ourselves from the exploitation of any means whatsoever. Then we can live a purely intellectual and spiritual life untainted by anything. . . . Every action could be a way of obtaining this. If it's not, it serves no end.

Palace of Desire

Life is above logic.

Adrift on the Nile

The first step on the ladder is the ability to concentrate fully. . . . By full concentration man merges into his essence. . . . Thus is affection cemented between you and the soul of existence. . . . It is the opener of doors to hidden treasures.

The Journey of Ibn Fattouma

Only the weak are afraid to live.

The Harafish

❦

If life has no meaning, why shouldn't we create a meaning for it? . . . Perhaps it's a mistake for us to look for meaning in this world, precisely because our primary mission here is to create this meaning.

Sugar Street

❦

To touch life's secrets is all that matters.

The Beggar

❦

A life dedicated to thought is certainly the most exalted type of life.

Palace of Desire

❦

Life's but a walking shadow on a summer's day, seeking shelter under the shade of a tree for an hour or so, and then is heard no more.

The Day the Leader Was Killed

❦

One must admit of some moral basis, otherwise the world would be transformed into a jungle.

The Journey of Ibn Fattouma

⟨❋⟩

If you've come to know what is not good for you, you may also think of it all as having been a sort of magical way of finding out what is truly good for you.

Miramar

⟨❋⟩

I do not regret the stages of life through which I have passed, for each stage has bestowed upon me its own particular light.

The Day the Leader Was Killed

⟨❋⟩

Sheikh Abd-Rabbih al-Ta'ih was asked whether life feels sad about anyone.

He replied: "Yes, if he is one of its faithful lovers."

Echoes of an Autobiography

⟨❋⟩

Existence itself is nothing but a composition of art.

The Beggar

⟨❋⟩

Confronting the misfortunes of life with patience and forbearance is a golden road to good fortune.

The Beginning and the End

❦

Once I said to Sheikh Abd-Rabbih al-Ta'ih, "I might welcome general exhaustion, but a single month's holiday makes me depressed."

He said, "Our nature is to love life and hate death."

Echoes of an Autobiography

❦

Life is for the benefit of the human being, otherwise his numbers wouldn't increase.

Mirrors

❦

The will to live is what makes us cleave to real life at times when, if it were left to our intellects alone, we would commit suicide.

Adrift on the Nile

❦

It's life itself that is important, not the meaning.

Adrift on the Nile

❦

Life appears to be a chain of struggles, tears, and fears, and yet it has a magic that enchants and intoxicates.

Echoes of an Autobiography

A full vessel does not produce hollow sounds.

The Beggar

Some people are preoccupied with life and others are preoccupied with death. As for me, my position is firmly fixed in the middle way.

Echoes of an Autobiography

I believe that love of life is half of worshipping and love of the afterlife is the other half.

Midaq Alley

Life gives opportunities for both reflection and repentance.

Arabian Nights and Days

Life consists of work, marriage, and the duties incumbent upon each person claiming human status. . . . The duty common to all human beings is perpetual revolution, and that is nothing other than an unceasing effort to further the will of life represented by its progress toward the ideal.

Sugar Street

※

And what is life? A passing game that a man plays with reluctance until he finds himself face to face with his ultimate fate.

Respected Sir

※

The best definition of life is that it is nothing.

Respected Sir

※

Life is a wonder. It is a sky laden with clouds of contradictions.

Akhenaten, Dweller in Truth

※

While there is life, there is no reason to despair.

Arabian Nights and Days

※

If I were not, I would wish to be.

Adrift on the Nile

※

Even a farce must continue right to the final act.

The Time and the Place

⚜

Life is made up of seasons, and to each its special flavor. Bless those who have loved life for what it is: God's world.

The Day the Leader Was Killed

⚜

Sudden disasters are always hard to believe, but life sometimes seems a series of sudden disasters. What matters is that you should find your way before it's too late.

Respected Sir

⚜

I've tried to solve part of the riddle, but have only succeeded in unearthing an even greater one.

The Thief and the Dogs

⚜

Isn't life amazing? In just one moment it wipes away sorrows that the oceans themselves could not wash off.

Respected Sir

⚜

Love for the secret of existence dies, so that existence itself loses all mystery.

The Beggar

If you look closely you'll discover an amazing similarity between a man and a kitchen. Each of them fills the belly with life.

Palace Walk

That is the way of life. You give up your pleasures one by one until there is nothing left, then you know it is time to go.

Naguib Mahfouz at Sidi Gaber

Why are we laughing . . . when life is a tragedy in every sense of the word?

Autumn Quail

Life is a flood of memories that pours forth into the sea of forgetfulness. As for death, it is the deeply rooted truth.

Echoes of an Autobiography

Life gives nothing except to those who are strong enough to take.

Miramar

The wisdom of life is the most valuable prize of our numbered days.

Mirrors

There is no life for us and no escape except by directing ourselves to the truth alone.

The Time and the Place

Life has only been created as a stage for the perform-ance of the wonders of Providence.

Respected Sir

Everything has youth and old age, it's the law of life.

Mirrors

I love life but will also welcome death when the time comes.

The Day the Leader Was Killed

Life is still good. And it will always be so.

Miramar

❀

We need to come back to life several times . . till we perfect it.

Autumn Quail

❀

Great life requires great sacrifices.

Khufu's Wisdom

❀

Life's train keeps moving down the tracks, even though death's station certainly lies ahead somewhere.

Palace of Desire

❀

Life can be summed up in two words: hello and goodbye.

Respected Sir

Love, Friendship,
and Happiness

❧

Our loved ones left us
Only words to remember.
O saddened heart,
Live not in grief,
For Osiris shall hear no pleas,
Nor will wailing
Bring back the dead.

Akhenaten, Dweller in Truth

❧

In leisure times I look out at the groups of birds on the
tree, happy in their flight and their singing. But their
singing and their flying is as nothing compared to being
close to the beloved.

Echoes of an Autobiography

Friendship is not based on self-interest or on other selfish motives. Friends simply enjoy each other's company. Anything can be imposed on people, including marriage, the one exception to this rule being friendship. For friendship can only develop when there is a sense of spiritual closeness.

Naguib Mahfouz at Sidi Gaber

They are two. By its strength the first created the other, and by its weakness the other created the first.

Echoes of an Autobiography

Let us be true to our world and devoted to our work, and may love, not law, control man's dealings with man.

Miramar

As you love, so will you be.

Echoes of an Autobiography

Next to the power of the almighty God, the power of love is the greatest.

Respected Sir

Love of the world is one of the signs of gratitude, and evidence of a craving for everything beautiful, and one of the distinguishing marks of patience.

Echoes of an Autobiography

The heart of the cruelest girl is like a block of ice: if a warm breath touches it, then it melts and pours as pure water.

Khufu's Wisdom

The mind may formulate specifications for the ideal woman however it likes, but love is an essentially irrational proceeding—like death, fate, and chance.

Autumn Quail

A word from the lips of the person we love is apt to make everything else seem insignificant.

Sugar Street

In the crevices of disasters, happiness lies like a diamond in a mine, so let us instill in ourselves the wisdom of love.

Midaq Alley

✻

It has been decreed that man shall walk staggering between pleasure and pain.

Echoes of an Autobiography

✻

People say that love is magic, and the magicians say that magic is love.

Rhadopis of Nubia

✻

Immortality is just a myth. Presumably love will be forgotten, like everything else in the world.

Palace of Desire

✻

A single beat from the heart of a lover is capable of driving out a hundred sorrows.

Echoes of an Autobiography

✻

Lovers often put their loved ones to a test, and if they only realized that that test is merely a trick and not serious, then their delight in their lovers would be increased.

Midaq Alley

A person who both loves and hates someone may find that the sorrow of parting obscures the hatred, leaving only the love.

Palace Walk

Love is stronger than everything.

Mirrors

A loving heart is the most reliable receptor of truth.

The Seventh Heaven

I came not because I loved but in order to love.

The Beggar

Between lovers there is discreet communion.

The Beginning and the End

From the beloved emanates a light in which all things appear to be created afresh.

Palace of Desire

Nothing save love is stronger than death.
Palace of Desire

Even the most wicked people will yield to the power of love, for love is stronger than the sword.
Akhenaten, Dweller in Truth

How can we be depressed when hearts have the capacity for love and our souls have the power of faith?
Midaq Alley

There is nothing like the magic of love to wipe away our cares.
Children of the Alley

Sheikh Abd-Rabbih al-Ta'ih said: We were in a cave conversing intimately, when a voice rang out, saying "I am love. Were it not for me the water would dry up, the air would become putrid, and death would strut about in every corner."
Echoes of an Autobiography

Love is stronger than evil itself.
Wedding Song

A treacherous man's love is as rotten and unhealthy as he is.
Miramar

To please you gives me reason to live.
The Beginning and the End

Affection is an ancient melody but seems marvelously fresh in each new rendition.
Palace of Desire

How beautiful it is to bid someone farewell with each of you holding the other in more esteem.
Echoes of an Autobiography

Every inch a person's body travels on the road of separation seems like miles to the heart.
Palace Walk

Blessed is the awakening that stirs beautiful memories in the heart.

Rhadopis of Nubia

The beloved may absent herself from existence, but love does not.

Echoes of an Autobiography

The words of the beloved lack the wisdom of philosophers and the glittering insights of fine authors, and yet they shake you to the core and cause springs of happiness to well up in your heart. This is what makes happiness a mystery baffling the most brilliant minds.

Palace of Desire

Strong words of love always please the ears, although they do not always appeal to the heart.

Midaq Alley

A woman in love is a plaything in a man's hand!

Children of the Alley

There is no alternative to love—just as there is none to
its denial.

Khufu's Wisdom

Only pain is stronger than love.

The Day the Leader Was Killed

Arrogance and love do not come together in one heart.

Arabian Nights and Days

Love is the key to the secrets of existence.

Echoes of an Autobiography

Love makes miracles happen.

The Harafish

In the past, I imagined you to be something that in
reality you have nothing in common with, so to hell
with all illusions.

Thebes at War

Love is like health. It is taken lightly when present and cherished when it departs.

Palace Walk

Love is a pure drop from the fountainhead of religion.

Palace of Desire

Fickle passions in the young can be cured, in wise men . . . they can't.

The Beggar

Love's an illness, even though it resembles cancer in having kept its secrets from medical science.

Palace of Desire

Love is fearless.

The Beggar

The language of orders has no place in love.

Rhadopis of Nubia

The breeze of love blows for an hour and makes amends for the ill winds of the whole of a lifetime.

Echoes of an Autobiography

The experience of love is precious even if it brings suffering.

The Beggar

The more people there are, the fewer who can live in friendship.

Adrift on the Nile

Singing is the dialogue of hearts in love.

Echoes of an Autobiography

These days only mules are lucky enough to be happy.

Wedding Song

Friendship is for life.

Adrift on the Nile

Remember, what love cannot cure, fear will not correct.

Akhenaten, Dweller in Truth

The affection of a friend endures. A girlfriend's passion is fleeting.

Palace Walk

How is it that happiness vanishes after being stronger than existence itself?

The Time and the Place

Unless you have faith in God, you'll never know real happiness.

The Beginning and the End

Does love give light only so as to reveal tragedy?

Wedding Song

If only money could buy happiness . . .

The Harafish

Happiness is short-lived and sorrow and pain outlive it.

The Beginning and the End

A slow and gradual change takes place as friendship turns to love just like the sudden budding of the leaves on a tree at the beginning of spring, something you can only see if you look very carefully.

The Day the Leader Was Killed

History and Politics

❦

History has laws more powerful than war or victory.
Mirrors

❦

Power alone is no guarantee of security . . . the only
guarantee of security is justice.
Naguib Mahfouz at Sidi Gaber

❦

The story of the attacks on the United States has a
moral, but sadly nobody seems to be heeding it. The
moral, or rather the most important of the many morals
to be learned from these disastrous events, is that power
alone is no guarantee of security.
Naguib Mahfouz at Sidi Gaber

Socialism is an expression of envy against the successful.

Mirrors

Politics isn't poetic idealism. It's realist wisdom.

Sugar Street

Revolutions are plotted by the clever, fought by the brave, and profited from by cowards.

Adrift on the Nile

Never scorn politics. It's half of life, or the whole of life if you consider wisdom and beauty to be above life.

Palace of Desire

If the system does not provide the means by which its application is guaranteed, then it won't survive.

The Journey of Ibn Fattouma

Every war has an end.

Palace Walk

Mankind of old faced absurdity, and escaped it through religion. And today again, man faces absurdity; but how can he escape this time?

Adrift on the Nile

If we don't confront terrorism with the anger it deserves, may the nation never live again.

Palace Walk

It would be better to remain without a role in a country which has one, rather than to have a role in a country which has none.

Autumn Quail

Life with no freedom has no value, and there is no freedom without sacrifice.

Mirrors

It's sad that a man should be transported such a long distance from his homeland to kill for someone else's sake.

Sugar Street

One might measure the strength of a democracy by the quantity of criticism that it is able to accept. Criticism becomes the daily bread on which any healthy democracy must feed.

Naguib Mahfouz at Sidi Gaber

The courageous soldier flies like an arrow toward his goal, without questioning the one who launched it.

Khufu's Wisdom

Nations gain their independence through the decisive actions of their sons.

Palace Walk

Though they aspire to be just and fair, monarchs are often oppressive.

Khufu's Wisdom

However disgusting the rat is, the sight of him in his cage is pitiable.

The Beggar

❦

War is an encounter between men, whose outcome is decided by the strong, while the weak suffer.

Thebes at War

❦

Politics corrupts the mind and heart. You have to rise above it before life can appear to you as an endless opportunity for wisdom, beauty, and tolerance instead of an arena for combat and deceit.

Palace of Desire

❦

No religion condones violence; no religion condones terrorism. There has never been a religion that spread its beliefs by holding a knife to people's throats in order to force them to join the faith.

Naguib Mahfouz at Sidi Gaber

❦

Man, unlike other creatures, always strives for freedom.

The Journey of Ibn Fattouma

❦

A people ruled by foreigners has no life.

Palace Walk

There can be no absolute guarantee that nuclear weapons will not be used in a moment of anger or of desperation. There can be no guarantee that nuclear weapons will be kept out of the hand of the unscrupulous, the irresponsible, or those whose stock in trade is terror.

Naguib Mahfouz at Sidi Gaber

There is nothing like politics to corrupt the mind.

Mirrors

The burdens of war mostly fall to the ordinary soldiers. . . . The commanders occupy a safer position planning and thinking things out.

Khufu's Wisdom

The Revolution has stolen the property of a few and the liberty of all.

Miramar

Has history ever known a king whose mind was carefree?

Khufu's Wisdom

Colonialism is the final stage of capitalism.

Sugar Street

Compassion, like power, is among the virtues of the perfect sovereign.

Khufu's Wisdom

In periods of unrest, the judicial system quails, and the police take precedence. Thus times of unrest are also times of police power. . . . The natural state of affairs is for the law to have the final say.

Sugar Street

When we're aware of our responsibility toward the masses, the search for personal meaning becomes quite insignificant.

The Beggar

An arm which can make money during the war can make double that in times of peace.

Midaq Alley

Democracy is the spirit of freedom. As such, it is not something to be granted by government alone, since unless it is deeply rooted, drawing nourishment from all sections of society, it is utterly worthless.

Naguib Mahfouz at Sidi Gaber

Treason is more powerful than the government and the people put together.

Autumn Quail

The nearest man comes to his Lord is when he is exercising his freedom correctly.

Echoes of an Autobiography

The essence of ruling, as the old Arab adage maintains, is justice.

Naguib Mahfouz at Sidi Gaber

War is a struggle to the death and mercy cannot be called on to prevent defeat.

Thebes at War

※

Woe to people under a ruler without a sense of shame.

Arabian Nights and Days

※

Nations survive and advance with brains, wise policies, and manpower—not through speeches and cheap populist agitation.

Palace of Desire

※

War, if not for a valid purpose, is nothing but slaughter and massacre.

Thebes at War

※

The meaning of nationhood has changed. . . . It's no longer a land with boundaries, it's a spiritual environment defined by opinions and beliefs.

Mirrors

※

It's strange: people always yearn to be free of government regulations, but they're delighted to load shackles on themselves.

Wedding Song

Freedom . . . is a responsibility which only the competent can be conversant with.

The Journey of Ibn Fattouma

The king is gone, replaced by countless kings.

Mirrors

When has politics ever left room for religion?

Naguib Mahfouz at Sidi Gaber

Necessity has its own laws.

Palace Walk

In politics, one of the last century's greatest human achievements was the liberation of the peoples of the Third World from imperialism, which in some areas was several centuries old. The uprisings that shook the world, especially at mid-century, were unprecedented. . . . They transported us forward into a new era, one of radically different political realities.

Naguib Mahfouz at Sidi Gaber

❦

History is very long-suffering. It will defend itself when all the other combatants have disappeared.

Autumn Quail

❦

I believe that the absence of punishment encourages crime and breeds evil among people.

Akhenaten, Dweller in Truth

❦

Anyone who neglects human rights, whether at home or at the ends of the earth, has neglected the rights of all mankind.

Sugar Street

❦

Every political system spawns its own culture. Democracies, though, have proved most able to sustain their cultures, to send out healthy sideshoots that flourish.

Naguib Mahfouz at Sidi Gaber

❦

Peace is yet more demanding of vigilance and readiness to do great things than war.

Thebes at War

Politics does not know final words.

Rhadopis of Nubia

Absurdity is the loss of meaning, the meaning of anything. The collapse of belief—belief in anything. It is a
passage through life propelled by necessity alone, without conviction, without real hope. This is reflected in the
character in the form of dissipation and nihilism, and
heroism is transformed into mockery and myth. Good
and evil are equal; and one is adopted over the other—
if adopted at all—with the simple motive of egotism, or
cowardice, or opportunism. All values perish, and civilization comes to an end.

Adrift on the Nile

Truth, Art, and Science

❦

Art is the interpreter of the human world. Besides that, some writers have produced works forming part of the international contest of ideas. In their hands art has become one of the weapons of international progress. There is no way that art can be considered a frivolous activity.

Sugar Street

❦

Beauty is just as convincing as the truth.

Rhadopis of Nubia

❦

Beauty is like a mirage that can only be seen from afar.

Palace Walk

The learned man seeks knowledge from the cradle to the grave—yet he dies an ignorant man.

Khufu's Wisdom

Literature that does not rise to the level of poetry—whether it takes the form of verse or prose—bears no relation to literature at all.

Naguib Mahfouz at Sidi Gaber

The writer's articles can generally be counted on to reveal the writer.

Adrift on the Nile

A play is a work of art, and art is a fantasy, no matter how much it borrows from the truth.

Wedding Song

Read the astronomy, physics, or other science texts, recall whatever plays and collections of poetry you wish and note the sense of shame which overwhelms you.

The Beggar

❊

Literature—great, humane literature—always sides with liberty and equality.

Naguib Mahfouz at Sidi Gaber

❊

Science has robbed art of everything. In science you find the rapture of poetry, the ecstasy of religion, and the aspirations of philosophy.

The Beggar

❊

I support absolute and unconditional freedom of the press, for I believe it is the lung that allows the nation to breathe. This is especially true in this day and age: information has become the most powerful weapon in the world. He who knows wins. The press plays a crucial role in this respect.

The press, however, must also be responsible and honest.

Naguib Mahfouz at Sidi Gaber

❊

Truly, beauty is a bewitching master who allows us a daily glimpse into the miraculous.

Rhadopis of Nubia

If your beauty works miracles, then why can it not cure me?
Rhadopis of Nubia

A work of art must be evaluated according to artistic criteria alone, not according to moral or social principles.
Naguib Mahfouz at Sidi Gaber

Real knowledge provides an ethical system in an age when morals are crumbling. It is manifested in a love of truth; in integrity in judgment; in a monastic devotion to work; in cooperation in research; and in a spontaneous disposition toward an all-enduring, humanistic attitude.
Adrift on the Nile

They often wonder about the secret of the flourishing of the theater. Do you know the secret? We have all become actors.
Mirrors

Poetry is my life and the coupling of two lines begets a melody which makes the wings of heaven dance.
The Beggar

If we can succeed in properly educating young people we need not worry about what they hear or see. They will be protected by the most powerful weapon in the world—the rational mind.

Naguib Mahfouz at Sidi Gaber

Embarrassment is the enemy of the art of acting.

Adrift on the Nile

Science brings people together with the light of its ideas. Art brings them together with lofty human emotions. Both help mankind develop and prod us toward a better future.

Sugar Street

Inwardly, art is a means of expurgation, outwardly a means of battle, incumbent on men born and reared in sin and determined to rebel against it.

Wedding Song

A popular saying is never without an enduring truth.

Mirrors

Mother Isis be praised that she endowed me with a mind that can perceive beauty in each of the colors that cover all things.

Khufu's Wisdom

True cultural development depends on the man, not the school.

Palace of Desire

The absurd has existed among us in abundance, even before it became an art.

Adrift on the Nile

Set off along the path of history in search of truth, a path that has no beginning and no end, for it will always be extended to those who have a passion for eternal truth.

Akhenaten, Dweller in Truth

It's always worthwhile to know the truth, no matter what it is or what effects people think it has.

Sugar Street

Beauty is not in the summer, nor in the winter, but in our love, and you will find the winter warm and gentle so long as the flame of love burns.

Rhadopis of Nubia

The relationship between political authority and culture has never been easy, whatever the political system. The political authority invariably craves or demands support, while the role of the intelligentsia is to act as the nation's conscience.

Naguib Mahfouz at Sidi Gaber

Art is an elevated form of entertainment and enhances life, but my aspirations stretch beyond art. What I want is to draw inspiration only from the truth.

Palace of Desire

The most significant and noteworthy events of human history can ultimately be traced back to some statement. The grand phrase contains hope, power, and truth. We proceed through life by the light of words.

Palace of Desire

A woman is utterly efficient in reaching her biological objectives using every means at her disposal. Whereas the artist has no objective but to express the essence of things, and that is Beauty. For Beauty is the sublime essence of that which creates harmony among all things.

Khufu's Wisdom

People need confidential advice, consolation, joy, guidance, light, and journeys to all regions of the inhabited world and of the soul. That's what art is.

Sugar Street

Just because you have changed doesn't mean truth has changed.

The Beggar

Be careful not to provoke the powerful, or gloat over the misfortune of those who have fallen into oblivion. Be like history, impartial and open to every witness. Then deliver a truth that is free of bias for those who wish to contemplate it.

Akhenaten, Dweller in Truth

The only true greatness lies in the life of learning and truth.

Palace of Desire

Between the slogans and the truth is an abyss in which we have all fallen and lost ourselves.

The Day the Leader Was Killed

It is an indication of truth's jealousy that it has not made for anyone a path to it, and that it has not deprived anyone of the hope of attaining it, and it has left people running in the deserts of perplexity and drowning in the seas of doubt; and he who thinks that he has attained it, it dissociates itself from, and he who thinks that he has dissociated himself from it has lost his way. Thus there is no attaining it and no avoiding it—it is inescapable.

Arabian Nights and Days

How beautiful it would be if man could devote his life to truth, goodness, and beauty. . . . The believer derives his love for these values from religion, while the free man loves them for themselves.

Palace of Desire

Only death can keep us from seeing the truth.
Akhenaten, Dweller in Truth

Truth, worship truth! Nothing in existence is more valuable or noble. Worship it and reject anything that might corrupt it.
Mirrors

Some old sage once said that in order to convince each other of the truth we may sometimes have to tell lies.
Miramar

The abode of scientists smells sweet; it is the smell of progress, of success.
Adrift on the Nile

One among them may spend twenty years solving an equation; and the equation will provoke new interest, and consume new lifetimes of research, and thus another firm footstep will be taken along the path of truth.
Adrift on the Nile

We must study the sciences and absorb the scientific mentally. A person who doesn't know science is not a citizen of the twentieth century, even if he is a genius. Artists too must learn their share of science. It's no longer just for scientists. Yes, the responsibility for comprehensive and profound knowledge of the field as well as for research and discoveries in it belongs to the scientists, but every cultured person must illuminate himself with its light, embrace its principle and procedures, and use its style.

Sugar Street

Science doesn't provide values, but it sets an example for courage. When classical determinism flagged, science adapted itself to probability, proceeding without looking back.

Mirrors

I have transferred from science to art a sincere devotion to the truth, a willingness to confront the facts no matter how bitter they are, an impartiality of judgment, and finally a comprehensive respect for all creatures.

Sugar Street

Science provides mankind with its magic, light, guidance, and miracles. It's the religion of the future.

Sugar Street

It is pointless to entertain hopes of communicating with people in a language other than the one they use, and we have acquired a new language, which is science. This is the only language in which we can articulate greater and lesser truths. For they are the old truths after all, once contained in the language of religion; and they must now be represented in the new language of man.

Adrift on the Nile

Science is a world language; our profession [as writers] deals with local riddles.

Mirrors

We have been created in order that we might endure the truth and stand up to it, receiving our share of pleasure and pain with the courage of believers.

The Journey of Ibn Fattouma

God created humans with the divine knowledge that
the boundaries of their discoveries could encompass
cloning; the scientist involved in cloning was himself
made by God, who is aware that His creations are
capable of scientific creativity.

Naguib Mahfouz at Sidi Gaber

Cloning is neither good or bad: it is a new scientific
experiment and one must not stand in the way of
scientific research. History bears testimony to the
imperative: every time mankind attempted to block
scientific progress it proved a mistake, from Galileo
to the present.

Naguib Mahfouz at Sidi Gaber

Science is the language of the intellect. Art is the language
of the entire human personality.

Sugar Street

Science has ascended the throne and the artist finds
himself among the banished entourage.

The Beggar

There is no survival for the human race except by eliminating the forces that exploit man's thought to enslave him, contriving conflicts that overcome his potential—a fast step to gather the world in a union based on wisdom and science, to re-educate the human being as a citizen of one world that provides him with security, and unleashes his creative powers to fulfill himself, shape his values, and proceed with courage toward the heart of truth concealed in this dazzling, mysterious universe.

Mirrors

Fear of progress is a moral not a scientific consideration. ...The atom is invaluable in science, in medicine, and in agriculture; progress must not be hindered just because humans are morally deviant. It is up to us to instruct mankind.

Naguib Mahfouz at Sidi Gaber

Our civilization is materialistic. Through science, it achieves unbelievable triumphs every day and lays the ground for man to dominate his world. But what's the use of owning the world and losing your self?

Mirrors

Death and the Afterlife

※

There's only one thing that's real—and that's death.

The Harafish

※

What can Death do to a heart that love has made immortal?

Khufu's Wisdom

※

Death is not the most atrocious thing we have to dread and . . . life is not the most splendid thing we can desire. . . . some facets of life are so rough and repulsive that death is sought instead and some so smooth and sustaining that immortality is desired.

Palace of Desire

We think of death as the ultimate tragedy . . . and yet
the death of the living is infinitely worse than that of
the dead.

Autumn Quail

She told him what had kept her away was Death. But he
rejected that excuse—for Death, he said, can never
come between lovers.

The Dreams

Death represents the one true hope in human life.

The Beggar

There is a death that seizes you when you are still alive.

Adrift on the Nile

O Lord, and I was delivered from the lances and the
chariots and the battles. So how can Death threaten me
in my dear, safe village, in the embraces of my spouse
and my mother and my children?

Voices from the Other World

Death is beautiful but maligned; without it, life would
have no value!

Mirrors

Fear does not keep death away, it keeps life away!
Children of the Alley

"I have come to hate myself."

"This may be a sign of a new birth."

"Or a new death."

"Let our conversation center on life not death."

"Death is also life!"

The Day the Leader Was Killed

How can we respond to the call of zeal and victory when
the heart is dead?

Palace Walk

The coming journey requires considerable preparation—
especially since it is eternal.

Khufu's Wisdom

Fear of death is the greatest curse to afflict mankind.

The Seventh Heaven

Time begets hope: it too brings about both death and life.

The Day the Leader Was Killed

One called out, "This is the end!"

A second shouted, "I see a gleam of an exit on the horizon!"

A third declared, "No matter what, there's no escaping the final reckoning."

The Dreams

Belief in the inevitability of death does not diminish our anguish when it arrives.

Palace of Desire

Many think it wise to make of death an occasion for reflection on death, when in truth we ought to use it to reflect on life.

Sugar Street

Why do we imagine that there exists a reality other than death in this world?

The Day the Leader Was Killed

❦

Death brings back memories of love and defeat.

Wedding Song

❦

No amount of questioning can bring about the dead.

The Time and the Place

❦

What could not be doubted is that Death is neither painful nor terrifying, as mortals imagine. If they knew the truth about it, they would seek it out as they do with aged wine, preferring it over all others.

Voices from the Other World

❦

Death is more merciful than hope itself. There is nothing surprising in this, for death is divinely appointed, while hope is the creation of human folly.

The Beginning and the End

Life will never be possible for you as long as you fear death.

Children of the Alley

Immortality is itself a death for our dear, ephemeral lives.

Khufu's Wisdom

Death often comes upon us without warning, like an earthquake.

Respected Sir

Death is inescapable. People die for one reason or another—or for none at all.

Palace of Desire

Death cheats the living.

The Thief and the Dogs

We die because we waste our lives in concerning ourselves with ridiculous things.

The Time and the Place

In a dead man's view, any kind of life is better than death.
Autumn Quail

Life and death were brothers. They were like one hand in the service of one hope. Life strengthened this hope with exertion, and death strengthened it with sacrifice.
Palace Walk

To us poor folk grief is a luxury we cannot afford.
The Beginning and the End

The dead can do without our loyalty.
Children of the Alley

We are hardly done with getting the house in order when there comes to us the call to depart.
Echoes of an Autobiography

The tomb is the threshold to perpetual existence.
Khufu's Wisdom

You will not attain the rank of the devout until you pass through six obstacles. The first of these is that you should close the door of comfort and open the door of hardship. The second is that you should close the door of renown and open that of insignificance. The third is that you should close the door of rest and open that of exertion. The fourth is that you should close the door of sleep and open that of wakefulness. The fifth is that you should close the door of riches and open the door of poverty. The sixth is that you should close the door of hope and open the door of readiness for death.

Arabian Nights and Days

Why is it that all beings disappear and nothing is left but dust?

The Time and the Place

We live and die by our strength of will. There's nothing more revolting than a victim. People who invite defeat. Cry out that death is the end of life. The ultimate truth. This outlook is the product of their weakness and their illusions. We are immortal.

The Harafish

An invalid clings to a moment of lucidity he fears intuitively may be almost his last.

Palace Walk

What can the families of the martyrs do? Should they spend the rest of their lives weeping? They weep and then forget. That's death.

Palace Walk

The happiest death for a man is after a pleasant evening to go to sleep and simply never wake up.

Miramar

A man spends much of his time on earth naked, but he can't cross the threshold of the grave naked, no matter how poor he is.

Midaq Alley

Tell me what meaning life has for us to seek or what delight there is to yearn for after death.

Palace of Desire

Countries live by the death of their heroes.

The Beginning and the End

Death itself is novelty.

The Day the Leader Was Killed

Why are we reminded of death so insistently, whatever we do?

The Beggar

For if only those suffering from loss would remember that Death is a void that effaces memory, and that the sorrows of the living vanish at the same speed with which the dead themselves disappear, how much toil and torment they could avoid for themselves!

Khufu's Wisdom

People who regard life and death as the same thing are really miserable creatures.

Autumn Quail

The friend to whom we seldom extend a welcome is death.
Echoes of an Autobiography

I am not afraid of death. I shall welcome it when it comes, but not before it is due.
The Day the Leader Was Killed

If it weren't for death, our life wouldn't have any value at all.
Autumn Quail

Death is now the last of the promised adventures. Its imminence helps alleviate one's burdens. It will reveal itself at some point and I shall gently say: Pluck the fruit now that it is at its ripest.
The Day the Leader Was Killed

Without realizing it . . . we're trying our death; we experiment with it time after time during our lives before death finally catches up with us.
Autumn Quail

Madmen rush unawares to meet their fate in accidents.
The Day the Leader Was Killed

What was this strange state . . . that wrested from a man all his will and ability, leaving him an absolute nothingness? So, this is death, death that advances with no one to repulse it, no one to resist it.
The Time and the Place

If you have sincerely loved the world, the Afterlife will love you warmly.
Echoes of an Autobiography

Faith, Ethics,
and Spirituality

❧

The rain falls on the earth, and does not disappear in space. Shooting stars gleam brightly for an instant, then plunge to extinction. The trees remain in their places, and never fly through the air. The birds circle around for a time, then return to their nests among the branches. There is a power at work, enticing everything to dance to a single rhythm.

The Harafish

❧

Whenever I pass over some test to the shores of peace and faith, I become more and more convinced of the wisdom with which He uses His power. In this way my afflictions always keep me in touch with His wisdom.

Midaq Alley

He who has lost his faith has lost life and death.
Echoes of an Autobiography

Who can judge a man's faith, when only God sees through our souls?
Miramar

Since ancient times, God has created evil people from the lions of pious ones.
Palace Walk

God is truth.
The Harafish

The spiritual world harbors as many unknowns as the world of matter. Mining it promises mankind great victories no less staggering than those of space travel. We only need to believe in a spiritual process as we do in the scientific process, and believe the complete truth is the meeting of two roads and not the end of one road.
Mirrors

Morals are the basis of good faith and successful social intercourse.

Naguib Mahfouz at Sidi Gaber

Meanings will only emerge to him who knocks at the door with sincerity.

The Journey of Ibn Fattouma

If it is true that man can be poor in God, so is it true man can be rich in Him.

The Thief and the Dogs

The body is a poor frame, sordid and amoral. It can fail and collapse with only an insect's sting. But the soul is immortal.

Akhenaten, Dweller in Truth

He who is humble about himself, God raises his worth; and he who exults in himself, God humbles him in the eyes of His servants.

Arabian Nights and Days

There is no joy so pure as the joy of worship.

Akhenaten, Dweller in Truth

Everyone thereon is transitory, except His face, and he who delights in the transitory will be beset by sorrow when that which delights him comes to an end. Everything is vanity except the worship of Him; sorrow and alienation throughout the world ensue from looking at everything but God.

Arabian Nights and Days

Inherited faith, doubt, atheism, rationalism, skepticism, then faith!

The Day the Leader Was Killed

For man to live a single second needs a great miracle from the Divine Power. The life of any man is a succession of divine miracles, and just think of the lives of everyone put together and the number of lives of all living creatures! Let us therefore thank God day and night. How insignificant our thanks are in the face of these divine blessings.

Midaq Alley

❧

I have always believed that those afflicted on earth are the closest favorites of God. He lavishes love on them in secret, lying in wait for them not far off, to see whether they are really worthy of His love and mercy.

Midaq Alley

❧

There is no way to bring back stability after it has died.

The Beggar

❧

To those who claim that creation is an attribute of God and God alone, I reply: justice, mercy, and generosity are also attributes of God. Should that stop people from being just, merciful, or generous? These attributes in God are one thing, in man another.

Naguib Mahfouz at Sidi Gaber

❧

Our religion is wonderful . . . but our life is pagan.

The Journey of Ibn Fattouma

❧

Holiness is bestowed only upon those who shun the world.

The Day the Leader Was Killed

On the question of Destiny . . . precaution cannot thwart Fate.

Khufu's Wisdom

We suffer yearnings without number that they may lead us to the yearning after which there is no yearning, so love God and He will make everything superfluous to you.

Arabian Nights and Days

If Fate really was as people say, then creation itself would be absurd. The wisdom of life would be negated, the nobility of man would be debased. Diligence and the mere appearance of it would be the same; so would labor and laziness, wakefulness and sleep, strength and weakness, rebellion and obedience. No, Fate is a false belief to which the strong are not fashioned to submit.

Khufu's Wisdom

If your soul is safe from you, then you have discharged its rights; and if people are safe from you, then you have discharged their rights.

Arabian Nights and Days

I asked Sheikh Abd-Rabbih, "What is the sign of unbelief?"
He replied without hesitation, "Discontentment."

Echoes of an Autobiography

Praise be to God, Whose existence has saved us from
frivolous play in the world and from perdition in the
Afterlife.

Echoes of an Autobiography

What must be studied . . . is the problem of religious
people who take the path of the absurd. They are not
lacking in faith, but still, in a practical sense, they lead
futile lives. How can this be explained? Have they mis-
understood the nature of religion? Or is it their faith
which is unreal, which is a matter of routine—a rootless
faith which serves merely to cover for the most vile
kinds of opportunism and exploitation?

Adrift on the Nile

What could happiness do to console a miserable,
disfigured, tainted soul?

The Beginning and the End

If the soul is not nourished by wisdom then it sinks to the level of the lesser creatures.

Khufu's Wisdom

The world of the spirit is incredible, more than the material world. . . . It's man's hope for true salvation.

Mirrors

Blessed is he who has but one thing to worry about . . . and whose heart is not preoccupied by what his eyes have seen and his ears have heard. He who has known God is abstemious about everything that distracts from Him.

Arabian Nights and Days

You create the germ of life
Within a woman, the seed of man.
You grant us the bounty of living
Before we see the light of your land.
Should you choose to cease your giving
The earth shall be in darkness,
In the silence of death.

Akhenaten, Dweller in Truth

※

The soul may lend a weak body power beyond its physical capabilities.

Akhenaten, Dweller in Truth

※

Faith is stronger than death, and death is nobler than ignominy.

Palace Walk

※

With the sage are to be found meanings that are hidden from the fleeting spectators.

The Journey of Ibn Fattouma

※

A believer's heart is his guide.

The Seventh Heaven

※

The longer a teacher lives, the more he learns.

Palace Walk

※

God loves those who love to commune with Him.

The Day the Leader Was Killed

O Lord, no matter how the soul suffers and is tortured, it goes on inventing and creating just the same.

Voices from the Other World

Nothing in the world can make up for the death of a young soul.

The Beginning and the End

Humanity as a whole needs some doses of Sufism. . . . Without it, life would lose its pleasure.

Autumn Quail

When all the spirits have become pure and free of any evil, everyone will hear the voice of God and we shall dwell in the truth.

Akhenaten, Dweller in Truth

God does not protect those who expose themselves to danger needlessly. He has commanded us not to put our lives in jeopardy.

Palace Walk

The atom is the flood. . . . Either we turn in truth to Almighty God, or else there will be 'clear destruction.'

Autumn Quail

God knows tomorrow, but the human being creates it.

The Seventh Heaven

God does nothing that is not wise, and wisdom is good.

Midaq Alley

A world without morals is like a universe without gravity.

The Thief and the Dogs

Faith is stronger than any other force on earth. . . .
Faith creates power and induces it.

Sugar Street

We need a new flood, the ark will carry the few decent people who will recreate the world!

Mirrors

No society can exist without an ethical base.
Naguib Mahfouz at Sidi Gaber

Attend lectures in all the different areas of learning without being tied down to a schedule or an examination. That way you can have a beautiful, spiritual life.
Palace of Desire

Forgiveness comes from God.
Palace Walk

It is true that many modern philosophies have tried to replace God with non-religiously derived ethical systems. . . . But a solely human search for truth and for right conduct is not the same as the guidance given by faith, since faith is given by God, and this is the essential difference between the two.
Naguib Mahfouz at Sidi Gaber

Belief is a matter of willing, not of knowing.
Sugar Street

The human spirit could be stronger than the most exercised muscles.

Akhenaten, Dweller in Truth

If you do not obey the devil, then God will lead you to your salvation.

Midaq Alley

One's soul is immortal.

Akhenaten, Dweller in Truth

We are in need of religion for religion's sake alone. . . . God alone gives value and gives value to existence. Without Him, life has no meaning, values have no meaning, and all effort is futile.

Naguib Mahfouz at Sidi Gaber

Life's Wisdom

He who deserts his monastery . . . must be content with the company of the profane.

Miramar

No matter what, the stages mankind traversed from the jungle to the moon cannot be ignored.

Mirrors

Happy is he who has fulfilled his task in the market or who has defied grief.

Echoes of an Autobiography

How could a hope of immortal kind be lost? It would mean that the annihilation of the world is possible and may, quite simply, happen.

Respected Sir

Ah, if only it were possible to go back in time as it is to go back in space.

Wedding Song

Sometimes a disaster will hit us in such a way as to lead us unawares along the right path.

Autumn Quail

Do not complain of the world. Do not search for wisdom behind those of its acts that are baffling. Save your strength for what is beneficial, and be content with what has been decreed. And if you are lured by an inclination toward melancholy, then treat it with love and song.

Echoes of an Autobiography

Why do people laugh, dance in triumph, feel recklessly secure in positions of power? Why do they not remember their true place in the scheme of things, and their inevitable end?

The Harafish

A dead man does not cry over having lost his sight.

Children of the Alley

When we have acute but temporary intestinal pain we forget our chronic eye inflammation, but once the intestinal distress is relieved, the pain in the eye returns.

Palace Walk

Even chaos is better than despair, and battling with phantoms is better than fear.

The Day the Leader Was Killed

Anyone who loses track of his past goes astray.

Palace of Desire

Two jewels are charged with looking after the golden door, saying to the one who knocks, "Come forward, for there is no escape." They are love and death.

Echoes of an Autobiography

When calamities accumulate they lose their sharpness and intensity.

The Day the Leader Was Killed

Don't say that philosophy, like religion, has a mystical character. It rests on solid, scientific foundations and advances systematically toward its objectives.

Palace of Desire

At times a person may create an imaginary problem to escape from an actual problem he finds difficult to resolve.

Palace Walk

Seth, in his wisdom, gives the sword to the strong master and glibness of tongue to the weak slave.

Thebes at War

"The real tragedy is that our enemy is at the same time our friend."

"On the contrary, it's that our friend is also our enemy."

The Thief and the Dogs

For the sake of the rose, the thorns get watered.

Palace Walk

Snakes are easier to live with than a lot of people.

Children of the Alley

Occasional failure to achieve one's aspirations does not undermine one's belief in them.

Respected Sir

The heroes of TV series are really lucky! They find the solution to their problems in no time!

The Day the Leader Was Killed

The long-lived may one day realize that he is longer-lived than the most beautiful symbols of life.

Echoes of an Autobiography

" 'If only' is the particle of anguish which has stupidly hankered after some illusory ability to change history."

"From the mystical point of view . . . it represents a denial of God's manifest will in history. What it does is to imbue things with futility and irrationality."

Autumn Quail

Just before we go to sleep we ought to say, 'Farewell,' because we may never wake up.

Palace of Desire

Sitting under a tree in a clear day is better than owning an estate.

Mirrors

Might does not make right. The mighty are those who can, when incensed, exert self-control.

The Day the Leader Was Killed

We grumble all the way down the Path of Light—so what do you think about while sliding down the Path of Darkness?

The Seventh Heaven

One day I tried to be detached, but the sighings of mankind invaded my seclusion.

Echoes of an Autobiography

The world is unaware of him who is unaware of it.

The Thief and the Dogs

You could not blame a proud wind for uprooting a dead, worm-eaten tree.

The Harafish

A downpour of rain starts with a few drops.

The Journey of Ibn Fattouma

I asked Sheikh Abd-Rabbih al-Ta'ih:

"When will the state of the country be sound?"

He replied, "When its people believe that the end result of cowardice is more disastrous than that of behaving with integrity."

Echoes of an Autobiography

The virtuous mind never dismisses wisdom even for a day, just as the healthy stomach does not renounce food for a day.

Khufu's Wisdom

All people seek refuge in the shade of the leafy tree, but when winter strips it bare they forsake it without regret.

Voices from the Other World

We sometimes go chasing something, and during the chase we come across the thing we are really looking for.

The Search

People with fine voices often have no ears to enjoy their singing.

Midaq Alley

The ideal is to believe and put your beliefs in action. To have nothing to believe in is to be lost forever. But to believe in something and nonetheless sit there paralyzed is sheer hell.

Miramar

What has befallen the earth that the lowly are made lords and the lords are laid low? The sovereigns are reduced to slaves, and the slaves are raised to sovereigns?

Voices from the Other World

With the inhalation of the universe and its exhalation, all joys and pains are in raptures.

Echoes of an Autobiography

Anything is better than nothing.

The Day the Leader Was Killed

If the inclinations of the inner self were to assume concrete form, crimes and acts of heroism would be life.

The Time and the Place

Everything is pledged for its due time.

The Journey of Ibn Fattouma

Some people are born to rule and others to serve.

Palace of Desire

To continue with worn-out traditions is foolishly dangerous.

Arabian Nights and Days

※

Rising at once recalls falling, strength recalls weakness, innocence recalls depravity, hope recalls despair.

Miramar

※

In the universe floats the will, and in the will floats the universe.

Echoes of an Autobiography

※

If you leave a dog in the kitchen with a piece of meat, can you imagine him promising not to touch it?

Palace of Desire

※

A man stalking prey finds the glistening full moon oppressive.

Palace Walk

※

If you are afflicted with doubt, then look at length in the mirror of your self.

Echoes of an Autobiography

Once the heart is disturbed how impossible for it to become cloudless!

The Time and the Place

It is necessary to have a certain amount of anarchy in order for the unmindful to awake from his state of indifference.

Echoes of an Autobiography

You win by alliance, and lose by defiance.

Akhenaten, Dweller in Truth

What counts is what you do, not what you think . . . and therefore I'm really no more than an idea.

Miramar

With a measure of wisdom, it is possible to derive lofty, sublime pleasures even from pain.

The Beginning and the End

God had created the beautiful stars to entice us to look upward. The tragedy is that one day they will look down from their height and find no trace of us.

Respected Sir

The heart is oppressed by any wisdom save that which sounds the death of all wisdom.

Adrift on the Nile

The wise man . . . is the one who knows where his foot will fall before he moves it.

Palace of Desire

'What is your heart like?' When I mentioned this to our master Shah Naqshaband, who was standing there, he suddenly stepped on my foot and I fainted. In my state of unconsciousness, I was made to see all of existence concentrated in my heart. When I came to, he said: 'If the heart is thus, how could it possibly be fathomed?' That is why we are told in the Hadith: *Neither can my earth or sky contain me. But the heart of my faithful worshiper can.*

The Day the Leader Was Killed

Time cuts life a sword. If you do not kill it, it kills you.

Respected Sir

Let's leave grief to time, which wears away iron and stone.

Miramar

Time and fate will never stand still.

The Harafish

Man will never suffer from a more lethal enemy than time.

Sugar Street

Even the strongest passions are assaulted, either gently or fiercely, by the passage of time.

The Harafish

Beware, for I have found no trade more profitable than the selling of dreams.

Echoes of an Autobiography

My dream is a gentle death.

Miramar

Up-down, death–resurrection, civilian–soldier, let the
world carry on. I'm preparing for another journey.

Mirrors

Bibliography of the Works of Naguib Mahfouz

All English titles are published by the American University in Cairo Press. Dates in parentheses refer to the first publication in Arabic.

Adrift on the Nile. Translated by Frances Liardet. 1993 (1966).

Akhenaten, Dweller in Truth. Translated by Tagreid Abu-Hassabo. 1998 (1985).

Arabian Nights and Days. Translated by Denys Johnson-Davies. 1995 (1982).

Autumn Quail. Translated by Roger Allen. Revised by John Rodenbeck. 1998 (1962).

The Beggar. Translated by Kristin Walker Henry and Nariman Khales Naili al-Warraki. 1986 (1965).

The Beginning and the End. Translated by Ramses Awad. Edited by Mason Rossiter Smith. 1998 (1949).

Children of the Alley. Translated by Peter Theroux.
2001 (1959).

The Day the Leader Was Killed. Translated by Malak
Hashem. 1997 (1985).

The Dreams. Translated by Raymond Stock. 2004 (2003).

Echoes of an Autobiography. Translated by Denys
Johnson-Davies. 1997 (1994).

The Harafish. Translated by Catherine Cobham. 1994
(1977).

The Journey of Ibn Fattouma. Translated by Denys
Johnson-Davies. 1992 (1983).

Khufu's Wisdom. Translated by Raymond Stock. 2003
(1939).

Midaq Alley. Translated by Trevor Le Gassick. 1985
(1947).

Miramar. Translated by Fatma Moussa Mahmoud.
Edited and revised by Maged el Kommos and John
Rodenbeck. 1998 (1967).

Mirrors. Translated by Roger Allen. 1999 (1972).

*Naguib Mahfouz at Sidi Gaber: Reflections of a Nobel
Laureate, 1994-2001.* From conversations with
Mohamed Salmawy. 2001.

Palace of Desire. Translated by William Maynard
Hutchins, Lorne M. Kenny, and Olive E. Kenny.
1992 (1957).

Palace Walk. Translated by William Maynard Hutchins and Olive E. Kenny. 1997 (1956).

Respected Sir. Translated by Rasheed El-Enany. 1998 (1975).

Rhadopis of Nubia. Translated by Anthony Calderbank. 2003 (1943).

The Search. Translated by Mohamed Islam. Edited by Magdi Wahba. 1987 (1964).

The Seventh Heaven: Stories of the Supernatural. Translated by Raymond Stock. 2005.

Sugar Street. Translated by William Maynard Hutchins and Angele Botros Samaan. 1997 (1957).

Thebes at War. Translated by Humphrey Davies. 2003 (1944).

The Thief and the Dogs. Translated by M. M. Badawi. Revised by John Rodenbeck. 1999 (1961).

The Time and the Place and other stories. Selected and translated by Denys Johnson-Davies. 1991.

Voices from the Other World: Ancient Egyptian Tales. Translated by Raymond Stock. 2002.

Wedding Song. Translated by Olive E. Kenny. Edited and revised by Mursi Saad El Din and John Rodenbeck. 1984 (1982).

Modern Arabic Literature
from the American University in Cairo Press